OUR FAVORITE FOODS

Ice Cream

by Christina Leaf

BLASTOFF! READERS 3

BELLWETHER MEDIA • MINNEAPOLIS, MN

Note to Librarians, Teachers, and Parents:

Blastoff! Readers are carefully developed by literacy experts and combine standards-based content with developmentally appropriate text.

Level 1 provides the most support through repetition of high-frequency words, light text, predictable sentence patterns, and strong visual support.

Level 2 offers early readers a bit more challenge through varied simple sentences, increased text load, and less repetition of high-frequency words.

Level 3 advances early-fluent readers toward fluency through increased text and concept load, less reliance on visuals, longer sentences, and more literary language.

Level 4 builds reading stamina by providing more text per page, increased use of punctuation, greater variation in sentence patterns, and increasingly challenging vocabulary.

Level 5 encourages children to move from "learning to read" to "reading to learn" by providing even more text, varied writing styles, and less familiar topics.

Whichever book is right for your reader, Blastoff! Readers are the perfect books to build confidence and encourage a love of reading that will last a lifetime!

This edition first published in 2020 by Bellwether Media, Inc.

No part of this publication may be reproduced in whole or in part without written permission of the publisher. For information regarding permission, write to Bellwether Media, Inc., Attention: Permissions Department, 6012 Blue Circle Drive, Minnetonka, MN 55343.

Library of Congress Cataloging-in-Publication Data

Names: Leaf, Christina, author.
Title: Ice Cream / Christina Leaf.
Description: Minneapolis : Bellwether Media, 2020. | Series: Our favorite foods |
Includes bibliographical references and index. | Audience: Ages 5-8. | Audience: Grades 2-3. |
Summary: "Simple text and full-color photography introduce beginning readers to ice cream.
   Developed by literacy experts for students in kindergarten through third grade"-Provided by publisher
Identifiers: LCCN 2019026788 (print) | LCCN 2019026789 (ebook) | ISBN 9781644871454 (library binding) |
   ISBN 9781618918215 (ebook)
Subjects: LCSH: Ice cream, ices, etc.--Juvenile literature.
Classification: LCC TX795 .L433 2020 (print) | LCC TX795 (ebook) | DDC 641.86/2--dc23
LC record available at https://lccn.loc.gov/2019026788
LC ebook record available at https://lccn.loc.gov/2019026789

Text copyright © 2020 by Bellwether Media, Inc. BLASTOFF! READERS and associated logos are trademarks and/or registered trademarks of Bellwether Media, Inc.

Editor: Kate Moening   Designer: Jeffrey Kollock

Printed in the United States of America, North Mankato, MN.

Table of Contents

Ice Cream on a Hot Day

The summer sun is blazing hot.
But you hear a familiar jingle.
The ice cream truck is near!

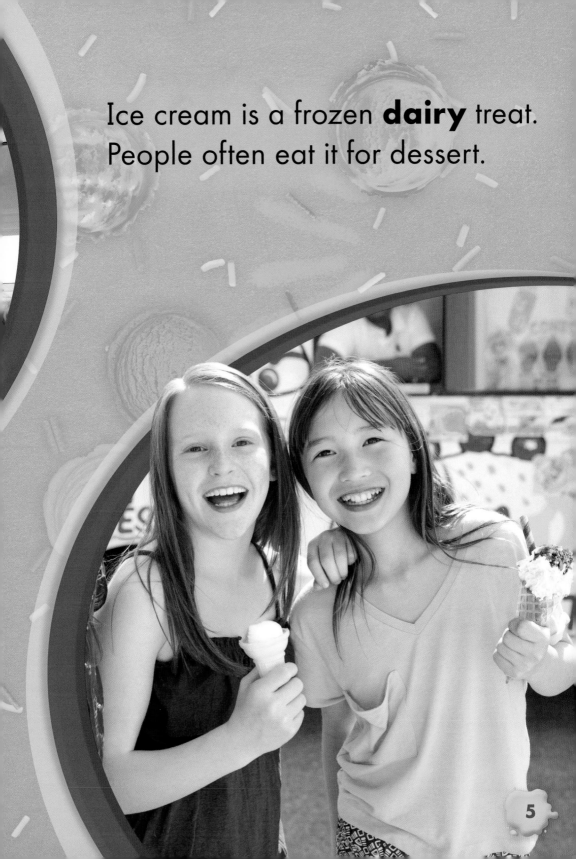

Ice cream is a frozen **dairy** treat. People often eat it for dessert.

Ice cream is milk or cream mixed with sugar. It often has added flavors like chocolate or strawberry.

How to Make Ice Cream

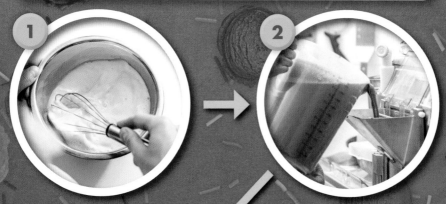

1 Mix ingredients

2 Add flavors

3 Churn while freezing

4 Ready to scoop!

6

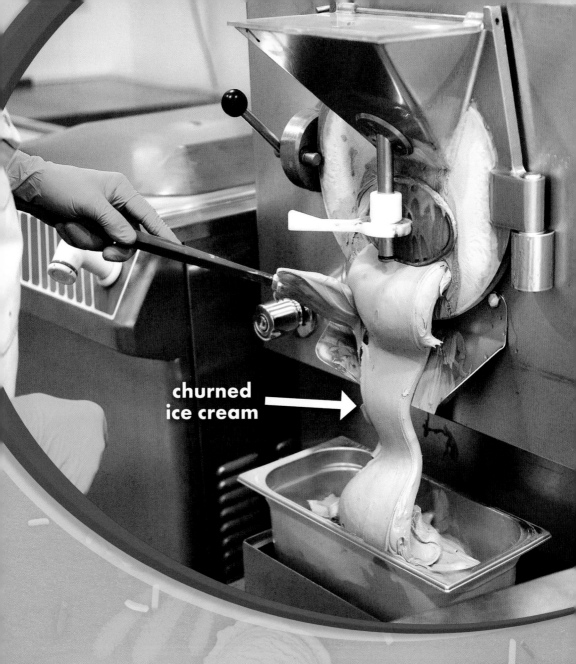

churned
ice cream →

Special machines are used to make ice cream. Paddles **churn** the ice cream while it freezes. This creates a smooth **texture**.

Ice Cream History

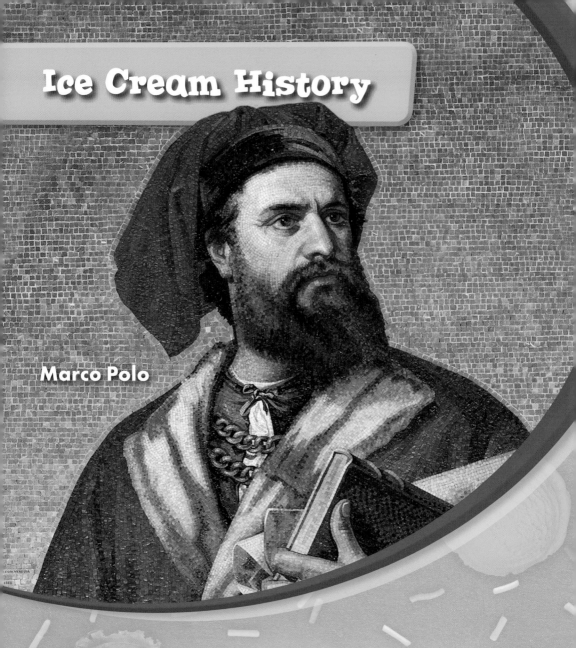

Marco Polo

Many people believe ice cream dates back to China in 200 BCE. A mixture of rice and milk froze in the snow.

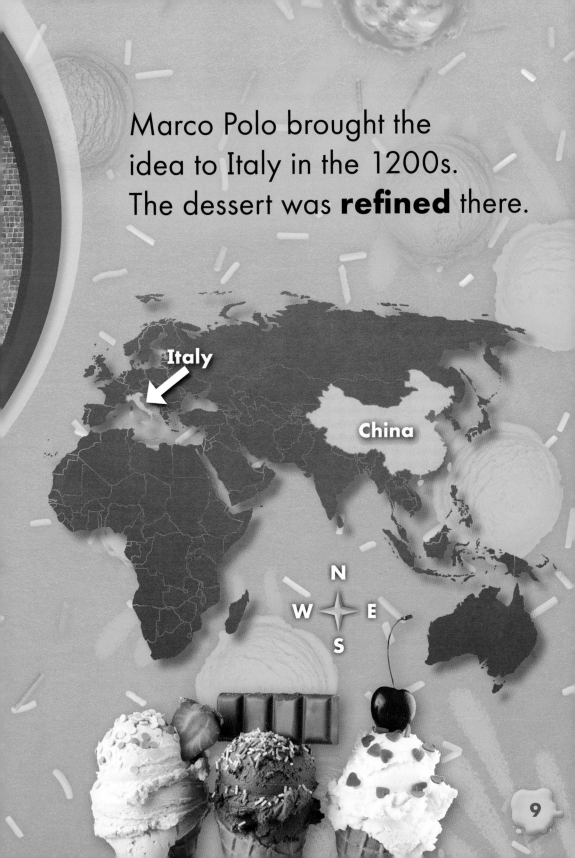

Marco Polo brought the idea to Italy in the 1200s. The dessert was **refined** there.

Italy

China

N
W · E
S

Ice cream was served in a Paris café in the late 1600s. The dessert was first recorded in the United States in 1744.

Ice Cream Timeline

200 BCE
Ice cream is likely invented by accident

1200s CE
Marco Polo brings ice cream to Italy

1744
Ice cream is first mentioned in the United States

ice house

Only the rich could afford
the treat. Sugar was costly.
Ice houses were, too.

11

No Churn Ice Cream

Have an adult help you with this homemade ice cream!

Tools

- mixer
- 2 large bowls
- whisk
- loaf pan
- spoon

Ingredients

- 14-ounce can sweetened condensed milk
- 2 teaspoons vanilla extract
- 2 cups heavy cream, cold
- pinch of salt
- optional: treats to mix in

Instructions

1. Whisk the condensed milk, vanilla, and salt together in a large bowl.

2. In another bowl, whip the cream with a mixer on medium-high for about 2 minutes. Peaks should form.

3. With a spoon, fold half of the whipped cream into the large bowl and combine.

4. Fold the mixture in the large bowl back into the whipped cream until it is blended.

5. Pour into a loaf pan, cover, and freeze for about 2 hours.

6. Mix in any flavors or treats.

7. Freeze again until solid, about 3 hours.

soda jerk

The first ice cream factory appeared in 1851. Factories made ice cream more common! By the end of the century, **soda jerks** served up sundaes. After the World's Fair in 1904, ice cream cones became favorite treats!

Ice Cream Today

Today, ice cream is everywhere! Hundreds of flavors fill grocery stores and ice cream shops. Flavors have candy, fruit, or even cookie dough mixed in!

People may add toppings like hot fudge or fresh fruit.

Ice cream also comes in milkshakes, root beer floats, and cakes. Pies can come **a la mode**.

pie
a la mode

hard ice cream

soft serve

Hard ice cream and smooth
soft serve are popular.
They come in cones or in cups.

mochi ice cream

kulfi

Ice cream looks different
internationally.
In Japan, a sticky dough
called *mochi* covers ice cream.
Indian *kulfi* is served on a stick.

Turkish ice cream is thick like taffy. In Germany, ice cream might look like spaghetti!

Ice Cream Around the World

Germany

spaghettieis

Iran

bastani

Thailand

rolled ice cream

Turkey

dondurma

19

Ice Cream of the Future

liquid nitrogen
ice cream

3D-printed
ice cream

Ice cream keeps changing.
Adding **liquid nitrogen** makes
a super smooth ice cream.
Some ice cream is **3D-printed**!
However it is made, ice cream
will always be a favorite treat!

Cake Batter Milkshakes

An adult can help you make these fun milkshakes!

Tools

- small bowl
- blender
- glasses

Ingredients

- 4 tablespoons heat-treated flour
- 3 tablespoons sugar
- 2 tablespoons dry milk powder
- pinch of salt
- 1/2 cup cold whole milk
- 1 cup soft vanilla ice cream
- 1 teaspoon pure vanilla extract
- optional: rainbow sprinkles
- optional: whipped cream

Instructions

1. Mix flour, sugar, milk powder, salt, and sprinkles in a small bowl.

2. Blend the dry mixture and the rest of the ingredients in a blender.

3. Top with whipped cream and/or sprinkles and enjoy!

Glossary

3D-printed—created with a 3D printer; 3D printers print layers of material according to directions from a computer.

a la mode—topped with ice cream

churn—to stir quickly

dairy—food that is made mostly from milk

ice houses—buildings in which ice is stored; ice houses kept food cold before refrigerators.

internationally—around the world

liquid nitrogen—a super cold liquid; liquid nitrogen must be kept colder than -321 degrees Fahrenheit (196 degrees Celsius).

refined—made more exact

soda jerks—people who serve drinks and ice cream at counters in restaurants or drugstores

texture—how something feels when you touch it

To Learn More

AT THE LIBRARY

Bader, Bonnie. *Curious about Ice Cream.* New York,
N.Y.: Penguin Young Readers Licenses, 2017.

Bailey, R. J. *Ice Cream: How Is it Made?.* Minneapolis,
Minn.: Jump!, 2017.

Heos, Bridget. *From Milk to Ice Cream.* Mankato,
Minn.: Amicus, 2018.

ON THE WEB

FACTSURFER

Factsurfer.com gives you
a safe, fun way to find
more information.

1. Go to www.factsurfer.com.

2. Enter "ice cream" into the search box
   and click 🔍.

3. Select your book cover to see a list
   of related web sites.

Index

The images in this book are reproduced through the courtesy of: MaraZe, front cover; stockcreations, p. 3, 14-15, 19 (spaghettieis); Hero Images, Inc./ Alamy, pp. 4-5, 5; progressman, p. 6 (Step 1); RossHelen, p. 6 (Step 2); Thanyarat Naiyanat, p. 6 (Step 3); Dusan Zidar, p. 6 (Step 4); joserpizarro, pp. 6-7; Wikimedia Commons, pp. 8-9; beats1, p. 9, 17 (bubble); Peter Lopeman/ Alamy, pp. 10-11; ODINTHEDOG/ Bellwether Media, p. 12; Ewing Galloway/ Alamy, p. 13; margouillat photo, p. 14; Charles Brutlag, pp. 16-17; artstore, p. 17; Elizaveta Shishova, pp. 18-19; StockImageFactory.com, p. 18 (kulfi); asianphotog/ Alamy, p. 19 (bastani); Studio Peace, p. 19 (rolled ice cream); Repina Valeriya, p. 19 (dondurma); Tahalefty, p. 20; ZUMA Press, Inc./ Alamy, p. 20 (bubble); Elena Veselova, p. 21; Foxys Forest Manufacture, p. 22.